Also by Carol Ann Duffy in Picador

The World's Wife
Feminine Gospels
Rapture
New Selected Poems
Mrs Scrooge
Love Poems
The Other Country
Another Night Before Christmas
The Bees
Wenceslas
Mean Time
Bethlehem
Ritual Lighting

AS EDITOR

Hand in Hand
Answering Back
To the Moon

The Christmas Truce

Carol Ann Duffy

with illustrations by David Roberts

PICADOR

First published 2011 by Picador

This edition first published 2014 by Picador
an imprint of Pan Macmillan, a division of Macmillan Publishers Limited
Pan Macmillan, 20 New Wharf Road, London N1 9RR
Basingstoke and Oxford
Associated companies throughout the world
www.panmacmillan.com

ISBN 978-1-4472-1844-9

3 5 7 9 8 6 4

A CIP catalogue record for this book is available from the British Library.

Manufactured in Belgium by Proost

Visit *www.picador.com* to read more about all our books
and to buy them. You will also find features, author interviews and
news of any author events, and you can sign up for e-newsletters
so that you're always first to hear about our new releases.

For Nia with love

The Christmas Truce

Christmas Eve in the trenches of France,
the guns were quiet.
The dead lay still in No Man's Land –
Freddie, Franz, Friedrich, Frank . . .
The moon, like a medal, hung in the clear, cold sky.

Silver frost on barbed wire, strange tinsel,
sparkled and winked.
A boy from Stroud stared at a star
to meet his mother's eyesight there.
An owl swooped on a rat on the glove of a corpse.

In a copse of trees behind the lines,
a lone bird sang.
A soldier-poet noted it down — *a robin*
holding his winter ground —
then silence spread and touched each man like a hand.

Somebody kissed the gold of his ring;
a few lit pipes;
most, in their greatcoats, huddled,
waiting for sleep.
The liquid mud had hardened at last in the freeze.

But it was Christmas Eve; *believe*; belief
thrilled the night air,
where glittering rime on unburied sons
treasured their stiff hair.
The sharp, clean, midwinter smell held memory.

On watch, a rifleman scoured the terrain —
no sign of life,
no shadows, shots from snipers,
nowt to note or report.
The frozen, foreign fields were acres of pain.

T hen flickering flames from the other side
danced in his eyes,

as Christmas Trees in their dozens shone,
candlelit on the parapets,
and they started to sing, all down the German lines.

Men who would drown in mud, be gassed, or shot,
or vaporised
by falling shells, or live to tell,
heard for the first time then –
Stille Nacht. Heilige Nacht. Alles schläft, einsam wacht . . .

Cariad, the song was a sudden bridge
from man to man;
a gift to the heart from home,
or childhood, some place shared . . .
When it was done, the British soldiers cheered.

A Scotsman started to bawl *The First Noel*
and all joined in,
till the Germans stood, seeing
across the divide,
the sprawled, mute shapes of those who had died.

All night, along the Western Front, they sang,
the enemies —
carols, hymns, folk songs, anthems,
in German, English, French;
each battalion choired in its grim trench.

So Christmas dawned, wrapped in mist,
to open itself
and offer the day like a gift

for Harry, Hugo, Hermann, Henry, Heinz . . .
with whistles, waves, cheers, shouts, laughs.

Frohe Weihnachten, Tommy! Merry Christmas, Fritz!
A young Berliner,
brandishing schnapps,
was the first from his ditch to climb.
A Shropshire lad ran at him like a rhyme.

Then it was up and over, every man,
to shake the hand
of a foe as a friend,
or slap his back like a brother would;
exchanging gifts of biscuits, tea, Maconochie's stew,

Tickler's jam . . . for cognac, sausages, cigars,
beer, sauerkraut;
or chase six hares, who jumped
from a cabbage-patch, or find a ball
and make of a battleground a football pitch.

I showed him a picture of my wife.
Ich zeigte ihm
ein Foto meiner Frau.
Sie sei schön, sagte er.
He thought her beautiful, he said.

They buried the dead then, hacked spades
into hard earth
again and again, till a score of men
were at rest, identified, blessed.
Der Herr ist mein Hirt . . . my shepherd, I shall not want.

And all that marvellous, festive day and night,
they came and went,
the officers, the rank and file,
their fallen comrades side by side
beneath the makeshift crosses of midwinter graves . . .

. . . beneath the shivering, shy stars
and the pinned moon
and the yawn of History;
the high, bright bullets
which each man later only aimed at the sky.

CAROL ANN DUFFY lives in Manchester, where she is Professor and Creative Director of the Writing School at Manchester Metropolitan University. She has written for both children and adults, and her poetry has received many awards, including the Signal Prize for Children's Verse, the Whitbread and Forward Prizes, and the Lannan and E. M. Forster Prize in America. In 2005 she won the T. S. Eliot Prize for *Rapture*. She was appointed Poet Laureate in 2009. In 2011 *The Bees* won the Costa Poetry Award, and in 2012 she won the PEN Pinter Prize.